THE ROAD TO BETHLEHEM

Study by David M. May
Commentary by Cecil Sherman

Free downloadable Teaching Guide for this study available at

NextSunday.com/teachingguides

NextSunday Resources
6316 Peake Road
Macon, Georgia 31210-3960
1-800-747-3016
©2018 by NextSunday Resources
All rights reserved.

TABLE OF CONTENTS

The Road to Bethlehem

HOW TO USE THIS STUDY

NextSunday Resources Adult Bible Studies are designed to help adults study Scripture seriously within the context of the larger Christian tradition and, through that process, find their faith renewed, challenged, and strengthened. We study the Scriptures because we believe they affect our current lives in important ways. Each study contains the following three components:

Study Guide

Each study guide lesson is arranged in four movements:

Remembering provides a frame of reference for the Scriptures.

Studying is centered on giving the biblical material in-depth attention while often surrounding it with helpful insights from theology, ethics, church history, and other areas.

Understanding helps us find relevant connections between our lives and the biblical message.

What About Me? provides brief statements that help unite life issues with the meaning of the biblical text.

Commentary

Each study guide lesson is accompanied by an additional, in-depth commentary on the biblical material. Written by a different author than the study guide, each commentary gives the opportunity for learners to approach the Scripture text from a separate but complementary viewpoint.

Teaching Guide

In addition to the provided study guide and commentary, *NextSunday Resources* also provides a *free* downloadable teaching guide, available at NextSunday.com. Each teaching guide gives the teacher tools for focusing on the content of each study guide lesson through additional commentary and Bible background information. Through teacher helps and teaching options, each teaching guide also provides substance for variety and choice in the preparation of each lesson.

NextSunday
Resources

STUDY INTRODUCTION

Happy New Year! With this greeting, you may be checking the date to see if you skipped a month or if, like Rip van Winkle, you slept through the last five weeks. If you are beginning this lesson on the first Sunday of Advent, you may be saying, "Ha, the publishers and author have made one big scheduling mistake if they think this Sunday is the beginning of the new year." It is no mistake. These lessons are the beginning lessons for the new year, that is, the new Christian Year. Advent, the celebrating of Jesus' first coming as an infant, has for centuries been the holiday signaling the beginning of the Christian calendar.

Virtually all of us use some type of calendar to organize and order our lives. So, the question is not whether we use a calendar, but whose we will use. As Christians, the journey we make through a year should first be organized around the same themes of faith that inspired our Christian ancestors. The year should reflect the biblical and historical stories that make each of our days special in their dedication to God. So, it is appropriate to begin our new year with an Advent celebration that takes us on a journey to Bethlehem.

During this Advent season, our journey is prepared not only by the Christian calendar but also by the writer of Matthew's Gospel. For any traveler willing to ponder, the Gospel writer has many insights on this journey. The first stop on this journey is Matthew's perspective on the proper balance between living for the future and living in the present. Session two finds us standing on a riverbank listening to John the Baptist: "Repent for the kingdom has come near" (3:2a). John's message is a continual call for reformation and transformation in our lives. The third session on this journey explores John's doubts about Jesus' identity. The fourth lesson brings us finally to the town of Bethlehem where all humanity is challenged by a newborn infant named Emmanuel. Session five is for all travelers who on the journey of faith encounter potholes and obstacles or who, like the character Christian in John Bunyan's *The Pilgrim's Progress*, find themselves in the "Valley of the Shadow of Death." It is a reminder that when Emmanuel is with us, there is always divine guidance for the journey.

Looking Forward and Looking Around

Matthew 24:36-44

Central Questions

- What do you anticipate for the future? What worries you about the future?
- How can we change our routines in order to stay alert for Jesus' return?
- How can we strengthen our hope in our Lord's coming?

Scripture

Matthew 24:36-44 But about that day and hour no one knows, neither the angels of heaven, nor the Son, but only the Father. 37 For as the days of Noah were, so will be the coming of the Son of Man. 38 For as in those days before the flood they were eating and drinking, marrying and giving in marriage, until the day Noah entered the ark, 39 and they knew nothing until the flood came and swept them all away, so too will be the coming of the Son of Man. 40 Then two will be in the field; one will be taken and one will be left. 41 Two women will be grinding meal together; one will be taken and one will be left. 42 Keep awake therefore, for you do not know on what day your Lord is coming. 43 But understand this: if the owner of the house had known in what part of the night the thief was coming, he would have stayed awake and would not have let his house be broken into. 44 Therefore you also must be ready, for the Son of Man is coming at an unexpected hour.

Remembering

I receive a quarterly statement about my anticipated retirement fund. With excitement and a little trepidation, I tear open the envelope and stare into my retirement future. The statement calculates my retirement for the year 2023. It used to seem a long way off, but financial planners tell us it is just around the corner, and one needs to think about the future.

Many Americans think a great deal about the future. Individuals save money, invest in the stock market, and buy all types of insurance to protect against a "bad" future. What church, business, or institution has not at some time had a long-term planning committee? We are a future-oriented society, many of us giving a great amount of thought to planning our personal lives, weddings, vacations, and retirement. News magazines and television programs are filled with predictions about the end of Social Security, the demise of rain forests, and the depletion of the ozone layer. Jesus' statement "Stay Awake" seems absurd for many of us who are fascinated with the future. We are wide awake and standing on tiptoes straining to prepare for the future. So what does this passage have to do with us and how we handle the future and live in the present?

Studying

Matthew is writing to people whose lives were concerned almost entirely with the present. Most agrarian people of the first century lived hand to mouth, scrambling to garner an existence from the rocky soil of Palestine. Rarely did these people think about the future. Like many poor people in our world today, many working peasants of the first century saw no future beyond the next day. Yet in 24:36-44, Jesus is nudging these people to think beyond their narrow view of the present and seriously consider the possibility that events they've relegated to the distant future could happen anytime.

This section of Matthew is a small part of Jesus' Apocalyptic Discourse (revelation) that begins in 24:1 and runs through 25:46. The ancients believed that God by way of prophets was continually revealing mysteries about the things above (heaven), the things below (hell), how everything began, or how everything will end (Rowland, 72). This section of Matthew deals with Jesus' revealing the mystery of the end.

As in Noah's day: Keep awake! (24:36-39) The language in these verses underscores what the end will be like. A key phrase is "that day." What is *that day*? Many ancient Jewish writers anticipated the day when God would intervene directly in the world. For Jesus, *the* day is when the Son of Man appears. For those wide awake, *the* day is one of excitement; but for those who have been sleeping and have no inkling of the Son of Man's coming, it is a day of horror.

These verses, like many that deal with endtime themes, are often misused and abused. In these passages, Jesus does not describe the end in detail. Jesus is more interested in cultivating an attitude about *how one should live* in anticipation of the end rather than in providing either a description of how to escape it or the details of its coming. Jesus turns to an Old Testament story, the story of Noah (Gen 6-9), in order to illustrate the attitude he hopes his followers will embrace as they look to the future.

> "Apocalyptic" is the transliteration of the Greek word that is literally translated "revealing." The English word apocalyptic, as used to define a genre of literature, comes from the Book of Revelation, sometimes called The Apocalypse. "Apocalypse" or "revelation" is the first word in that book.

The story of Noah and the ark taught to children today was also a popular story in the ancient world. Jesus uses this story to compare people's attitudes in his day with those in Noah's day. In this comparison, Jesus reveals the proper attitude for looking to the future and living in the present.

The comparison with the Noah story is about neither the weakness of that time nor God's wrath upon wickedness. It is about the *uneventfulness* of that time. Noah's day, just as the one Jesus anticipates, was an era marked by common practices like eating, drinking, and marrying. There were no incredible signs or supernatural events, just the nitty-gritty features of everyday life. Then, in the midst of the routine, a colossal flash flood takes away the unsuspecting. Those awake, Noah and his family, remained and were spared.

As in Jesus' day: Keep awake! (24:40-41) In order to stress the point of his comparison, Jesus uses an agricultural image. He portrays field workers planting or weeding and women grinding meal. Suddenly, in the midst of the ordinary, one is swept away as the victims in Noah's day. The reference to Noah corrects a typical misreading of verses 40-41, which is to misunderstand those "taken" as those who are saved (Moody, 546). The ones snatched away are not awake: Within the routine of life, they are persons who possess no sense of the future. The ones who remain are, like Noah's family, awake and saved. They always anticipate the extraordinary presence of God. The call to keep awake, however, is a summons to more than wide-eyed passive waiting. It requires the responsibility and accountability highlighted by Jesus' parable in the following verses.

Wakeful responsibility (24:43-44)
Jesus cultivated watchfulness, anticipation, and readiness for his return by sharing this startling metaphor. The Son of Man will come like a thief in the night (see 1 Thess 5:6-8). Jesus often used shocking images to shatter a person's preconceived notions, and this picture *is* shocking. The good shepherd becomes the sneaky thief! It is strange to imagine Jesus coming by stealth in the dark of

In Jesus' endtime speeches, he often refers to a Son of Man who seems distinct from Jesus himself. Who is this Son of Man? This title is used in various ways in the Gospel, but is found only on the lips of Jesus. Although it seems as if Jesus is speaking about another, the early church clearly associated the returning Son of Man with Jesus himself.

night and digging through the clay bricks of a home to steal what little property a person might possess.

After getting over the initial shock of Jesus as robber, the original listeners would have identified with the violated householder. Nodding their heads in empathy they could say, "We know how it feels to be robbed when you least expect it." The point is not only that they should be awake, but also that while awake they could do something to discourage a would-be robber. As Jesus puts it, an awake householder "would not have let his house be broken into (24:43)." To be awake for the coming of Jesus is to show responsibility in the interim.

With the stress of everyday existence and the Roman imperial army occupying the land, the future did not seem to exist for the subjugated Jews of the first century. Jesus tried to broaden their view by giving them a glimpse of imminent events so that the drudgery of the present day might give way to an excited antici- pation. Jesus' call was not merely a call to an anticipation that demanded nothing more than to have one's eyes glued to the sky, waiting for the Son of Man's return. It was a summons to respon- sibility in the Son of Man's absence.

The whole of Matthew's Gospel teaches that our responsibility is to pattern our lives after Jesus. We must do what Jesus did. His was not a self-centered lifestyle, but a life of feeding the hungry, giving drink to the thirsty, welcoming strangers, clothing the naked, taking care of the sick, and visiting prisoners (Mt 25:31-46). In other words, and using Jesus' imagery, being caught unaware means that when the Son of Man comes, we are grinding grain only for ourselves. We must be awake and found grinding grain for each other.

Understanding

People today tend to seek the spectacular for excitement. The fascination with UFOs, television shows highlighting the para- normal, and people seeing visions in trees or on sides of buildings, stimulates the imagination and conversation. Only an invasion in the Mideast and high oil prices will get most Americans excited about the return of Jesus. The everyday and ordinary can dull our senses and tempt us to reflect sleepily that "this is the way it has always been and always will be." The writer of 2 Peter experienced the same situation when people said, "Where is the promise of his coming? For ever since our ancestors died, all things continue as they were from the beginning of creation!" (3:4).

Jesus' first coming in the midst of ordinary people and difficult times should inspire us to anticipate a similar return. Jesus' words remind us to maintain an eagerness for his return, even after 2000 years and even in the routineness of everyday life. For in the ordinariness of everyday existence is the extraordinary possibility of the Son of Man's return.

These words of Jesus are also a warning to any of us who plan our futures in self-centered ways. When we focus our energy, time, and resources on *our* long-range plans, *our* retirement funds, and the security systems for *our* lives, we can miss those who presently need us. To anticipate Jesus' return is to believe that we will be found faithfully serving others. It is the thrill of being prepared for Jesus' return. What a great loss we may experience if, after spending years planning our personal futures, Christ returns when we're on the verge of retirement. All such plans can easily be swept away (Lk 12:13-21), while any ministry "to the least of these" is eternally worthwhile (Mt 24:31-46).

What About Me?

Long before the Boy Scouts' motto, "Be prepared," the Christian banner was "Keep Awake." To keep awake means to be prepared by actively engaging in the work of the absent Son of Man. We need to look around to see what the Son of Man would be doing in our community or church if he were himself individually present. The church is the body of Christ. What are we, the hands, arms, and legs of Christ, doing in Christ's absence?

A stained-glass window of one of the ancient churches in Europe depicts a person on bent knee, obviously in prayer. This glass mosaic is unusual in that the person praying has one eye covered and one eye wide open. The window theologian wanted all those who gazed at it to know the attitude we need as we enter and leave the church. We pray and anticipate, but we are wide awake in all our activities, believing that the Lord will come.

Perhaps we should be challenged to use more of the language of our ancestors in faith, who after every Lord's Supper would utter *maranatha*, "our Lord come." Advent is the time for us to renew our hope until "our Lord comes."

What biblical stories do you teach to children?

Resources

R. Alan Culpepper, "Maranatha," *Mercer Dictionary of the Bible*, ed. Watson E. Mills et al. (Macon GA: Mercer University Press, 1990).

Calvin Mercer, "Son of Man," *Mercer Dictionary of the Bible*, ed. Watson E. Mills et al. (Macon GA: Mercer University Press, 1990).

Dale Moody, *The Word of Truth* (Grand Rapids: Wm. B. Eerdmans Publishing, 1981).

Paul Redditt, "Apocalyptic Literature," *Mercer Dictionary of the Bible*, ed. Watson E. Mills et al. (Macon GA: Mercer University Press, 1990).

Christopher Rowland, *The Open Heaven* (New York: Crossroad, 1982).

LOOKING FORWARD
AND LOOKING AROUND

Matthew 24:36-44

Introduction

Our title suggests the lesson will be "forward looking." Since Advent usually signals Christmas is near, we do some translation and come out with something like this:

(1) Advent means Christmas is near.

(2) Christmas is the time when we celebrate the birth of Jesus.

(3) "Jesus is coming," when studied during Advent, means we are getting ready for the coming of the Christ Child. I looked in my dictionary and found "Advent" defined this way: "the coming of Christ at the incarnation" (*Webster's New Collegiate Dictionary*, Springfield, MA: G. & C. Merriam Co., 1980, 17).

Are we getting ready for something that has already happened? Jesus has already been born. This text is not about the coming of Jesus as a baby born to Mary in Bethlehem. It is about Jesus coming again.

Many strange people have said many strange things about the Second Coming. Predictions have come and gone. Calculations about "when" Jesus will return have been fantastic and wrong. All this is in spite of the plain word of Jesus, "about the day and hour no one knows" (24:36). Most thoughtful preachers and lay people have backed away from the subject.

Matthew's gospel does not back away from the Second Coming. Chapters 24 and 25 are about last things. Chapter 24 opens with a question from the disciples: "Tell us, when will this be, and what will be the sign of your coming and of the end of the age?" (24:3). A series of descriptions and signs about what is to happen at the "end of the age" and how we can live intelligently in anticipation of it follows the question. Our text comes from the "parables and monitory pictures" that alert Matthew's readers to the way they should act in anticipation of Christ's Second Coming (*The New Interpreter's Bible*, Vol. VIII, Nashville: Abingdon Press, 1995, 444). We are "readers." The more "at home" we are in this world, the more this text has to say to us.

So our study is not "looking forward" to the birth of the baby Jesus in Bethlehem. This study is about another of Jesus' comings, the Second Coming.

I. Nobody Knows When, 24:36.

The disciples of Jesus probably speculated about *when* Jesus would return and *when* the Kingdom would be established. It is a normal way of thinking. Consider some of the ways we talk about *when*.
• When will the stock market go up or down?
• When will my team win the World Series?
• When will the kid at loose ends find himself?
• When will my old car "give up the ghost?"

In Christian circles, talk of when Jesus will come again has surfaced with almost predictable regularity. A preacher reads the "signs of the times" and comes up with a formula that calculates when the end will come. Events prove the preacher wrong, but that does not deter the next preacher from making another prediction.

Jesus warned us about trying to predict the Second Coming. He said, "But about that day and hour no one knows, neither the angels in heaven, nor the Son, but only the Father" (24:36). Since we can't predict it, some people dismiss it. This text tells us that too is a mistake. In fact, two ideas are held in tension in this lesson:

(1) Don't spend your time worrying about or trying to predict the Second Coming. Work steadily and be ready to give account about the assignments Jesus has given all his disciples.

(2) Give serious thought to the future. To make no provision for the world to come is a mistake.

II. God Has Come in History, 24:37.

"For as the days of Noah were..." (24:37a). This is a wake-up call. It is as if Jesus were saying, "You think God is remote and distant. You think that God coming and interrupting your calendar is impossible." But it's not.

(1) In Noah's time, God moved. God tired of sinful people living as if God didn't exist or was powerless. "They knew nothing until the flood came and swept them all away, so too will be the coming of the Son of Man" (24:39). Those people were oblivious to God. For them, the idea that God would break into the routine of life was out of the question. Jesus was saying that God moved in the time of Noah. Only Noah and his family knew God well enough to anticipate what was happening. Noah and his family were "Looking Forward and Looking Around."

(2) At the birth of Jesus, God moved. Most people missed it. Events at Bethlehem were "small potatoes" on the big screen. Rome or Athens was where the news was being made. Two thousand years later, Caesar, though still a figure of some consequence, shrinks in size next to Jesus. Knowledge of the baby from Bethlehem has grown until a great part of the world's population now claims him as their Lord and Savior.

God has moved twice. Noah and his family, Joseph and Mary, a few shepherds and Wise Men were "Looking Forward and Looking Around." They caught what God was doing. The rest? God came near, and they missed it.

III. Routine Can Anesthetize, 24:38-39.

Of the people who lived during the time of Noah, Jesus said, "For as in those days before the flood they were eating and drinking, marrying and giving in marriage until the day Noah entered the ark, and they knew nothing until the flood came and swept them all away..." (24:38-39). "Eating and drinking, marrying and giving in marriage" are what people do in every generation. These are the routines of life. Though cultures differ, the pattern is the same. The pattern goes on. We grow old and die. Our children grow old and die. Their children do the same. The beat goes on.

We begin to see life as a kind of cosmic metronome—beating, beating, beating. Jesus is telling us that this routine can put us to sleep. Routine can become an anesthesia. We quietly give up on the idea of God's intervening, Jesus' coming. We never renounce the faith. We just define it as duty in this world. We leave thoughts about the Second Coming unspoken.

Noah anticipated God. The rest were surprised. Noah was "Looking Forward and Looking Around." He had an eye for the sin of his time. He had a feel for God's response to it. He was useful to God and a model to us. Noah was not anesthetized by the routine of life.

IV. One Will Be Taken and One Will Be Left, 24:40-42.

Jesus paints a picture of what the Endtime will be like. "Two will be in the field; one will be taken and one will be left. Two women will be grinding meal together; one will be taken and one will be left" (24:40-41).

(1) This is not a "Rapture" scene. The word does not appear in the Bible. Jesus' description of the Endtime is straightforward. Christ will come and a Great Judgment will divide humankind. Then Eternity will begin. Some will be blessed, others will be cursed. The picture of "one will be taken and one will be left" is a way of describing judgment. A more popular picture of the same event is in Matthew 25:31-46.

(2) This is perhaps the most unnerving part of this passage: The two men in the field look alike, seem to be alike. The two women grinding at the mill look alike, seem to be alike. But when Jesus comes, that which is hidden from us will become clear: One is saved and one is lost (*The New Interpreter's Bible*, Vol. VIII, 446). We cannot anticipate the results of Judgment. It would seem that all who profess faith in Jesus would be saved, but some people don't follow their profession with an appropriate lifestyle. These are guesses about Judgment, and we would do well to leave Judgment to God.

(3) Matthew divides the house two ways. We like to divide everything three ways. There's your side and my side and then there's a middle position that is probably nearer the truth than either of "our" positions. But Matthew is not familiar with modern systems of moral grading. With amazing consistency, he tells of wise and foolish, faithful and evil, sheep and goats.

So what happens to our Black, White, plus Gray? It's not in the text. Somehow God is going to take into account the good in bad people and the bad in good people and come out with a two-way division of the house. I don't understand it, but this is true to Matthew's text.

V. The Call to Be Ready, 24:43-44.

The text ends where it began. "About that day and hour no one knows..." (24:36a). Then "if the owner of the house had known in what part of the night the thief was coming..." (24:43). We get this message: We can't time it. But we may miss this one: The Second Coming will be when we don't expect it.

Jesus used an illustration that I've had a hard time comprehending. He compares his Second Coming to the coming of a thief in the night. The illustration is obvious: If we knew when the thief was coming, then we would intercept the thief. But in the thief's favor is our not knowing when or where he is going to strike. It's a strange way to think, but Jesus often used illustrations that stretched the minds of his audience. So what do we get from the thief story? The Second Coming will be at a time we least expect, "Therefore you...must be ready, for the Son of Man is coming at an unexpected hour" (24:44).

How do I stay ready for the Second Coming of Christ? The question is not answered plainly until the very end of the two chapters on Last Things. Carefully read Matthew 25:31-46. According to Matthew, what will count at Judgment is the way we have acted toward hurting, helpless, needy people. Amazingly, a profession of faith is not mentioned. Do not take this text in isolation and build a doctrine of salvation on it. But to forget this text in a doctrine of salvation would do violence to the Scriptures and the clear warning of Jesus as recorded by Matthew. Paul's theology in Romans (especially chapters 3-6) needs to be put alongside Matthew's theology in our text. The combination of the two gives balance.

Notes

Notes

2

TRANSFORMED BEING AND REFORMED LIVING

Matthew 3:1-12

Central Questions

- Whom would you describe as prophetic?
- When have you experienced the powerful presence of God at work in the world?
- How is the word repentance misused and misunderstood? From what do you need to repent?
- From what does the church need to repent? What would you like to see reformed?

Scripture

Matthew 3:1-12 In those days John the Baptist appeared in the wilderness of Judea, proclaiming, 2 "Repent, for the kingdom of heaven has come near." 3 This is the one of whom the prophet Isaiah spoke when he said, "The voice of one crying out in the wilderness: 'Prepare the way of the Lord, make his paths straight.'" 4 Now John wore clothing of camel's hair with a leather belt around his waist, and his food was locusts and wild honey. 5 Then the people of Jerusalem and all Judea were going out to him, and all the region along the Jordan, 6 and they were baptized by him in the river Jordan, confessing their sins. 7 But when he saw many Pharisees and Sadducees coming for baptism, he said to them, "You brood of vipers! Who warned you to flee from the wrath to come? 8 Bear fruit worthy of repentance. 9 Do not presume to say to yourselves, 'We have Abraham as our ancestor'; for I tell you, God is able from these stones to raise up children to Abraham. 10 Even now the ax is lying at the root of the trees; every tree therefore that does not bear good fruit is cut down and thrown into the fire. 11 "I baptize you with water for repentance, but one who is more powerful than I is coming after me; I am not worthy to carry his sandals. He will baptize you with the Holy Spirit and fire. 12 His winnowing fork is in his hand, and he will clear his threshing floor and will gather his wheat into the granary; but the chaff he will burn with unquenchable fire."

Remembering

Slogans are found everywhere in print, on television, over the radio, and by way of the computer. It seems a good marketing strategy to grab an audience's attention with catchy, memorable phrases: "Just Say No." "A mind is a terrible thing to waste." "When you care enough to give the very best." "Just do it."

Slogans, much a part of our culture, have their own unique outlet of proclamation: the bumper sticker. Rare is the car that does not have a 3 x 11-inch sticker proclaiming some belief, view of life, or comment on driving habits. Bumper stickers affixed to automobiles also tell a great deal about the drivers or owners of the vehicles and their views of the world. Bumper sticker slogans let us see what others proclaim to believe.

Slogans so saturate our world that when we read the words of John the Baptist, "Repent, for the kingdom of heaven has come near (3:2)," our apathy and cynicism surface. We have heard it before; it seems just another religious slogan. Yet, these words were not composed in some Fortune 500 company board room or in a religious denominational office. They were not designed for bumper stickers or calendars. A wild-eyed prophet inspired by God's Spirit drove these words into the hearts of his listeners. These words are powerful. They challenge listeners today to be transformed and to seek ways of changing the world around them.

Studying

When, Who, Where, What? (3:1) Many of us were taught in a writing class that an article's first paragraph should answer the questions who, when, where, what, and why. Matthew seems to have had such a writing class. In 3:1, he answers all of the questions except why, which he answers in verse 2.

Matthew moves from the story of Jesus' birth in chapter 2, jumps several decades, and abruptly introduces a new story line and a new character, John the Baptist. Matthew begins by answering the *when* of these events. The answer, "in those days," is a little ambiguous for modern readers, but for Matthew's readers "those days" were the days of Roman rule.

The bottom line in "those days" was always the same: taxation, tribute, colonial oppression. Everyone knew someone in debt or in prison, or a person who had lost land, been threatened, beaten, or seized, or someone who had simply disappeared. Oppression hung in the air of Judea.

"Those days" also defined a time of division among Jews. The Jewish elite and Jerusalem priests were set over against the peasant population and the lower-level country priests such as Zechariah, John the Baptist's father. What the Romans did not take in tribute and taxation, the Jewish Temple and its overseers did. Only meager resources were left for the peasants and the poor Jewish priests.

In the region of Judea, Romans ruled, and Roman puppet rulers were in Galilee (Herod Antipas) and in Trachonitis (Herod Philip). Both of these rulers were descendants of Herod the Great.

All the events recorded in 3:1-12 occurred in the wilderness, a place filled with potential and risk. As the children of Israel had learned, the desert was both a place of exile and also a place of purifying and refining. The desert was as fire to ore, and one could come out of the desert experience refined like gold.

In "those days" and into such a place comes John the Baptist, literally John "the Dipper." There is no question about how we are to understand the role of John. If he looks like a prophet (camel hair clothing, 3:4a), and eats like a prophet (locusts and wild honey, 3:4b), and sounds like a prophet ("Repent," 3:2), then he must be a prophet.

Prophets usually stood out in crowds. Their dress, actions, and words fascinated some and repelled others. Like a moth drawn dangerously close to a fire, the crowds are always dangerously drawn to prophets. Some considered them mad, and they may have been, but we need to understand the madness. Contained within these fragile human beings was the revelation and spirit of the Creator God (Lk 1:80). They were called to proclaim a message, usually an unpopular one. They had a good reason to be a little "crazy." Yet in their divine madness, they commanded attention from people—peasant and privileged, government rulers and religious leaders. When they declared their message, one might reject it or accept it, but one could never ignore it. John was a prophet, a person proclaiming a message that could not be ignored.

The Revival Message: Why? (3:2) John made an incredible impression on the people of his day. Jesus said about him, "Truly I tell you, among those born of women no one has arisen greater than John the Baptist" (Mt 11:11a). *Why* such high praise from Jesus for a lonely man shouting "Repent, for the kingdom of heaven has come near" in the desert? Because this message was an invitation for change and is not to be confused with a mere slogan.

The message John proclaimed is only seven words in Greek. Yet it was a call that became the hub of a wheel that sent a revival movement, the movement of God, spinning through Israel. You may have heard of revivals lasting two weeks or several months, but in a very real way this revival movement begun by John and Jesus continues *today*. We continue in a revival that began 2000 years ago with John the Baptist's words.

Those who joined this revival movement did so with the imperative *repent* (*metanoia*) echoing in their ears. While false prophets often arose and declared new kingdoms just around the corner, none coupled their messages with the need for individuals to do anything personally about it. It would happen with or without them. John's message, however, was unique. He invited people to participate actively in the change that the movement of God was bringing. All who repented could participate.

Too often we misunderstand the depth and context of this original call for repentance. Today it is often equated with feeling sorry for moral failures. John was proclaiming much more. Repenting for John also meant more than turning around and going in a different direction. In asking people to repent, John and Jesus were essentially saying, "Give up your way of being Israel, your following of particular national and political aims and goals," asking the people to trust in God's way for the direction and movement of their lives (Wright, 254). Such a definition of repentance and the acceptance of it through baptism (3:6) meant joining this movement of God. Nothing in their world could or would be the same again.

Those who accepted this message, the newly baptized, had gone into the water as exiles from God and come up from the water as a new Israel with a new beginning. It is no coincidence that John's message and baptism took place in the wilderness. Exile from God was over, and a new Israel born.

Renewal and restoration carried incredible consequences for change and reformation. If forgiveness is granted in the wilderness, and not in the Jerusalem Temple where it was expected, then the old methods and rituals are unnecessary. The new is here. If people are gathering in the wilderness and pledging allegiance to God, then a new exodus has occurred, and a new land exists for a new citizenry.

Josephus, a Jewish historian during the time of John the Baptist, could not overlook this solitary prophet living and preaching in the wilderness. He noted John's influence among the people and Herod Antipas's fear of him.

If traditions related to the covenant are gone, then new relationships are established and a new definition exists for the people of God. These reformations take place because new members in the movement of God are called to active participation.

Understanding

"Repent" is not a word we often use today. It seems part of a bygone era, now relegated to cartoon characters who carry it painted on placards. Yet, it is the heart of the message of John and Jesus. It is a call for change. When repentant people change, there are new ways of doing business, new aims and goals, and a new allegiance. This new allegiance to the Kingdom of Heaven, or the movement of God, is demonstrated in active service.

One writer captures this feeling in these words, "True repentance spends less time looking at the past and saying, 'I'm sorry,' than to the future and saying, 'Wow!'" (Buechner, 96). The wow of John's message is that life oriented toward God's goals means reform is breaking out: lifestyles, social structures, and institutions are changing. They are changing because we have changed.

What About Me?

Do we need to repent during this Advent season? Do we need to repent for following goals that have nothing to do with the movement of God? To be a part of the movement of God is to be an agent for change. The movement of God is exhibited not only by our proclamation, but also by the reformation we bring into the world. The beginning of the new Christian year is a good time to reflect upon the goals for which we strive. What have been the motivating factors in our lives during the last year? How is our repentance demonstrated in the reforms we are making?

The movement that John began was one of renewal and restoration. Now is the time to evaluate those areas, not only in our personal lives, but also in our churches. How do the people of God today need reform and renewal? Perhaps the burnout and lack of enthusiasm in some corners of Christendom today is due to the pursuit of the wrong aims and goals. How might renewal reorient us toward what is truly crucial?

For example, in John's day Israel was called to renounce nationalistic hopes and the violence associated with ridding the country of Romans. This was not the way of the Kingdom of God. What would happen if we also abandoned goals that have nothing to do with the kingdom way? What would happen if we were to "bear fruit worthy of repentance," to actively pursue the goals of God's Kingdom, to seek God's rule in our lives?

> What in your life needs renewal and reformation?

Resources

Amnesty International On-line, http://www.amnesty.org/ (15 April 1998).

Frederick Buechner, *Wishful Thinking: A Seeker's ABC* (San Francisco: HarperSanFrancisco, 1993).

J. Bradley Chance, "John the Baptist," *Mercer Dictionary of the Bible*, ed. Watson Mills et al. (Macon GA: Mercer University Press, 1990).

Walter Harrelson, "Desert," *Mercer Dictionary of the Bible*, ed. Watson Mills et al. (Macon GA: Mercer University Press, 1990).

John H. Hayes, "Repentance," *Mercer Dictionary of the Bible*, ed. Watson Mills et al. (Macon GA: Mercer University Press, 1990).

N. T. Wright, *Jesus and the Victory of God* (Minneapolis: Fortress Press, 1996).

TRANSFORMED BEING
AND REFORMED LIVING

Matthew 3:1-12

Introduction

Moving further into the season of Advent, this session looks back to Bethlehem. Reflecting on the past is a necessary step as we travel further down our personal road to Bethlehem.

The last time Jesus came, someone helped the people get ready for him. It might be that the prophet who helped them recognize and welcome Jesus could also help us.

Bible scholars do not agree about John the Baptizer. Some believe he was more competitive with Jesus than the gospels would have us believe. His followers competed with Jesus' disciples (Jn 3:25-30). These scholars contend that the gospel writers made it seem John supported the ministry of Jesus more than he actually did.

More traditional Christian teaching holds that Isaiah foretold the coming of John the Baptizer (Is 40:3; Mal 4:5). John was sent of God for the specific purpose of announcing Jesus. John did what he was supposed to do and quietly receded into Herod's prison and Jewish history. The truth probably lies between these two views. John did not anticipate Jesus would turn out as he did (Mt 11:2-6). It is sad to think of the fearless prophet, sitting in Herod's prison, alone and wondering if the one he announced was really God's anointed Messiah. I can imagine John the Baptizer at peace with the growing ministry of Jesus; it is harder to see John's disciples pleased that "he must increase, but I must decrease" (Jn 3:30).

God gave John the Baptizer a message that helped a spiritually hungry people be receptive to Jesus. Some of John's disciples left John and followed Jesus (Jn 1:35-37). Some of John's audience left him and went after Jesus (Jn 4:1). John was faithful to his task. (Lk 7:24-35). We need to study John the Baptizer in preparation for our own meeting with Jesus. He prepared people for Jesus once; he can do it again.

The Prophet Attracts a Crowd, 3:1-6.

Matthew does not prepare his readers for John. Chapter two closes with Jesus an infant in Nazareth. Chapter three opens with Jesus as an adult, but Jesus was not the center of attention. The commanding presence was a prophet who was leading a revival in the Judean wilderness.

The Judean wilderness is forbidding country. This land is somewhat similar to that of West Texas or New Mexico. I recall a flight from Atlanta to Phoenix. It was a clear day and I was seated by the window. In the amazing way of the West, the land was green and farms were dotted here and there. Then the land became more rough and dry. Trees were sparse. Finally, we were over near desert with no vegetation in sight. Then out of nowhere, there appeared a long green strip of trees and cultivated land. We were over New Mexico, and the green and vegetation was alongside the Rio Grande River. As fast as it appeared, it was gone and the desert was everywhere. Keep this picture in your mind as you think of the setting for the revival of John the Baptizer. Desert is all around, with a river Jordan running through it. It was remote, lonesome country, but this setting was significant. It was in the Wilderness that God was close to Israel. Purity and purpose were given to them in the Wilderness. Going to the Wilderness and finding God would not surprise a knowledgeable Jew.

John was preaching, "Repent, for the kingdom of heaven has come near" (Mt 3:2). Matthew tells us, "This is the one of whom the prophet spoke..." (3:3a). The prophet was Isaiah (Isa 40:3).

The preacher was not smooth or sophisticated. He was like the wilderness around him. His food and clothing advertised that he had rejected the soft life. He was different and his religion was different.

The effect of his ministry was electrifying. "The people of Jerusalem and all Judea were going out to him, and all the region along the Jordan" (3:5). Hunger in the soul for some honest religion made common people leave home and crop to see and hear this different preacher. John didn't want their money. He wasn't concerned with their sacrifices or temple tax. He was beyond the rule-ridden ways of the Pharisees. This man had a ring of authenticity; he was genuine. Ordinary people saw the difference between John and the Pharisees. The size of the crowd in so remote a place spoke volumes. John said something they longed to hear; the Pharisees and Sadducees left people hungry in the heart.

John's message was plain: "Confess your sins." With John, baptism followed confession. This baptism would seal the convert "from the eschatological judgment to come" (*The New Interpreter's Bible*, Vol. VIII, Nashville: Abingdon Press, 1995, 157). John's baptism was a purging of the soul in preparation for the Messiah. So the people were dipped under the waters of the Jordan. What kind of soul cleansing do we need in preparation for Jesus?

II. A Prophet Confronts Sick Religion, 3:7-10.

While John was preaching and baptizing, he looked up and "saw many Pharisees and Sadducees coming for baptism" (3:7a). Many would have welcomed the Pharisees and Sadducees to baptism, but John saw them with a prophet's eye. Listen to what he told them:

(1) "You brood of vipers! Who warned you to flee from the wrath to come?" (3:7b). Normally, Pharisees and Sadducees did not act in concert. They usually opposed each other. But when the established order of religion was threatened, both groups had a vested interest in keeping things as they were. When these two groups appeared before John, they were as one. This would become their practice when they opposed Jesus.

John saw both Pharisee and Sadducee as an evil presence in Jewish life. They were to the religious life of the Jews as a viper was in a children's playground.

(2) "Do not presume to say to yourselves, 'We have Abraham as our ancestor'" (3:9a). William Barclay offers this insight on Jewish thought when Jesus lived:

To the Jew Abraham was unique. So unique was he in his goodness and in his favour with God, that his merits sufficed not only for himself but for all his descendants also...So the Jews believed that a Jew simply because he was a Jew, and not for any merits of his own, was safe in the life to come (*The Gospel of Matthew*, Vol. 1, Philadelphia: Westminster Press, 1958, 39).

John's message was a jolt to conventional theology. John says that we can't secure eternal life from the goodness or the faith of our parents or grandparents.

(3) "Even now the ax is lying at the root of the trees; every tree that does not bear good fruit is cut down and thrown into the fire" (3:10). This idea is reinforced by "Bear fruit worthy of repentance" (3:8). Matthew does not explain what "good fruit" is, but Luke does. When John the Baptizer's strong preaching produced both fear and desire to change, the people cried out, "What then should we do?" (Lk 3:10). And the Baptizer said:

• If you have two coats, share with him who has none.
• If you have food, share with him who has none.
• To tax collectors he said, "Collect no more than the amount prescribed for you" (Lk 3:13).
• To soldiers he said, "Do not exhort money from anyone by threats or false accusations, and be satisfied with your wages" (Lk 3:14).

These were the "fruits" John was looking for in a changed life. Repentance can cleanse us from old sins; but getting clean is not the end of it. Bearing fruits must follow.

For a long time, people have tried to have a changed heart without a changed life. We wish for a "feel good" religion that frees us of guilt, but John wanted more. He preached repentance from sin, and he pushed for "fruits." Jesus did the same thing. He called for repentance, and a changed life—a fruit bearing one. John the Baptizer's list of "good fruit" is similar to Matthew 25:31-46. Jesus said we must feed the hungry, cloth the naked, and visit the imprisoned. This is the fruit bearing that Jesus requires.

III. A Prophet Predicts a New Order, 3:11-12.

John the Baptizer was in between a Christian and an Old Testament Jew. He has been called the last of the Old Testament prophets. What the prophets saw dimly was the lasting vision of John. He recognized Jesus, baptized him, and stepped offstage. Jesus said of him, "I tell you, among those born of woman no one is greater than John; yet the least in the kingdom of God is greater than he" (Lk 7:28). Maybe that says it all. John climbed as high as the religion of Moses could take him. Jesus would take over from there and move to the next level. What did John see?

(1) "One who is more powerful than I is coming after me; I am not worthy to carry his sandals" (3:11). This statement must have surprised John's audience. Does this mean there is someone greater? And if there is someone greater, who is he? Where can we find him? If John's revival was preliminary (and it was big, otherwise, the Pharisees and Sadducees would not have noticed); what was the main attraction going to be? "One who is more powerful..."

(2) "I baptize you with water...He will baptize you with the Holy Spirit and fire" (3:11). What kind of baptism would that be?
• *Fire*. The baptism of Jesus would purify as fire burns away the dross, making all that remains pure and clean.
• *Spirit*. The baptism of Jesus would be like a fresh breath of God. When God breathed the first time, human beings became "a living being" (Gen 2:7b). We now have that possibility again. What was damaged in Eden, Jesus will repair.

(3) "His winnowing fork is in his hand, and he will clear his threshing floor and will gather his wheat...but the chaff he will burn" (3:12). John the Baptizer must have anticipated rejection from the Jewish religious establishment. The covenant made at Sinai was broken and there had to be something new. It would be the Church. Pentecost would give a baptism of the Spirit. The chaff was thrown away and the wheat was refined and became the staple for the Bread of Life.

John the Baptizer stood on one of those breaking points in time. The old was passing away and a new creation was emerging. It was like the first rays of dawn. The glory that would become clear at noon was still first morning light. John saw faintly what Paul would see in full day. Jesus made the difference.

Someday the tired, worn rags of our religion will be replaced. What we see now only by faith, we will see by sight. If this stirs your spirit as it does mine, maybe we are anticipating, dreaming, hoping, faithing the next order. This has to be a milepost on the Road to Bethlehem.

Notes

Notes

3

A PUZZLING
MESSIAH

Matthew 11:2-11

Central Questions

• How has your view of Jesus changed since you were a child?
• What confuses people about the identity of Jesus?
• How have we reconstructed Jesus in our own image? In what ways can we attempt to see Jesus as he really was? As he really is?

Scripture

Matthew 11:2-11 When John heard in prison what the Messiah was doing, he sent word by his disciples 3 and said to him, "Are you the one who is to come, or are we to wait for another?" 4 Jesus answered them, "Go and tell John what you hear and see: 5 the blind receive their sight, the lame walk, the lepers are cleansed, the deaf hear, the dead are raised, and the poor have good news brought to them. 6 And blessed is anyone who takes no offense at me." 7 As they went away, Jesus began to speak to the crowds about John: "What did you go out into the wilderness to look at? A reed shaken by the wind? 8 What then did you go out to see? Someone dressed in soft robes? Look, those who wear soft robes are in royal palaces. 9 What then did you go out to see? A prophet? Yes, I tell you, and more than a prophet. 10 This is the one about whom it is written, 'See, I am sending my messenger ahead of you, who will prepare your way before you.' 11 Truly I tell you, among those born of women no one has arisen greater than John the Baptist; yet the least in the kingdom of heaven is greater than he.

Remembering

One Christmas my three-year-old nephew put together a twenty-five piece puzzle. His system was unusual. Instead of organizing all the pieces on the table, he took only one piece out of the box and used it as his starting point. Then he selected another piece out of the box and try it for fit. If it did not work, he tossed it back into the box and tried another. Systematically he tried piece after piece. When a piece fit, then the process began all over again. Finally, after all the pieces were in place, he smiled and clapped his hands, "A train! It's a train!"

As John sat in prison, his disciples brought him pieces of a puzzle about Jesus. At the time John baptized Jesus, there were not so many pieces. Yet Jesus had spoken life-changing words (Mt 5-7) and performed mighty deeds (Mt 8-10). John was trying to understand this Messiah. The pieces of the puzzle were fitting together but the picture was quite different from John's expectation.

All of us paint our own portrait of Jesus. Usually, we construct our understanding through our experiences, our church, and our reading of the Bible. We may feel satisfied with our portrait of Jesus. John's dilemma, however, may challenge our satisfaction. Are we seeing and hearing Jesus for who he really is? Have we forced some pieces together and even improvised in order to get a picture we like? Especially at this time of Advent, with the many images of Jesus being portrayed, it helps to take a fresh look at this person called Jesus, the Messiah.

Studying

Who are you? (11:2, 3) Reading Matthew's Gospel, we might wonder why John the Baptist had questions about Jesus. Had he not already baptized Jesus? Had John not confessed to Jesus that he needed to be baptized by him (3:14)? Had he not witnessed the heavens opening and the voice from heaven: "This is my Son, the Beloved, with whom I am well pleased" (3:16, 17)? We might think that John should have easily recognized Jesus as the

Messiah, but before we judge John too harshly, we must remember the age in which he lived.

In the first century, there was no unified belief about who the Messiah would be or what the Messiah would do. We often have an image of a unified ancient Judaism in which everyone knew how to recognize the Messiah. Nothing could be farther from the truth. Several competing versions of basic Jewish beliefs existed. The Pharisees, Sadducees, John the Baptist and his disciples, Jesus and his disciples, and others were different groups within Judaism. For example, the Essenes, a radical community of Jews living near the northwest corner of the Dead Sea, believed that there would be two coming messiahs, one kingly and the other priestly. Because of such diversity among the Jews, it is not surprising that differing messianic expectations arose.

John thought he knew what the Messiah would be like and had publicly declared the Messiah's role. He believed that the "coming one" would be an ax-carrying messiah (3:10). John understood the role of the messiah as chopping down, chopping up, and then setting on fire all the unholy aspects of this world. The messiah John proclaimed was the avenger of God's wrath. This avenger was kindling an unquenchable fire (3:12). Imagine John's surprise when his disciples informed him that Jesus was saying, "Do not resist an evildoer. But if anyone strikes you on the right cheek, turn the other also (5:39)" and "Love your enemies and pray for those who persecute you (5:44)." No wonder John was confused. The picture on his puzzle box did not match the pieces he was putting together.

> "The four Gospels—Mark, Matthew, Luke, and John—emerged as literary portraits of Jesus, written between A.D. 60 and 90 to keep the oral tradition of Jesus alive....The portraits of Jesus left by the communities of faith help us, as twentieth-century followers of Jesus, design our own portrait." (Bridges, 8, 17)

Showing and telling (11:3-5) When the disciples of John challenged Jesus with the question, "Are you the one who is to come, or are we to wait for another?" Jesus refrained from giving them a direct answer. Life is rarely a true or false test. Jesus does not give easy answers. He challenges you to think and observe for yourself. Jesus challenged John's disciples to "hear and see," then answer their own question. Jesus does, however, point them in the right direction.

In verse 5, Matthew uses the actions and words of Jesus to reveal Jesus' true identity and the correct understanding of his role as Messiah. If John and his disciples can see and hear, observing both his deeds and his speech, they will recognize his identity, but not without challenging some of their traditional beliefs about the Messiah.

Matthew uses Jesus' actions to reveal his character. Jesus heals the blind (9:27-31), lame (9:1-8), and deaf (9:32-34). As foretold in the Old Testament, these actions are associated with the expected Messiah (Isa 35:5, 6). Jesus also acts in ways not associated with Old Testament messianic traditions (Michaels, 175). He cleanses the lepers (8:1-4) and raises the dead (9:18-26).

The identity of Jesus is also revealed in his words, which are good news to the poor. In the ancient world, the poor were not only those economically disadvantaged, but also any who could no longer maintain their honor and station in life. Persons who experienced illness, loss of land, or death of family members were also considered poor. In Matthew, the Sermon on the Mount (Mt 5-7) is good news to the displaced and powerless. Jesus' words assured them that they were blessed. Imagine the shock. The crowd must have thought, "No one has ever called us blessed; we are mere nobodies in this world. We are blessed?" And Jesus' words would continue to encourage them: "There is a place for the weakest, meekest, and saddest person in the movement of God. It is in

> The concept of messiah is necessarily refashioned in light of the history of Jesus. The Jewish idealizations of a Davidic messiah, whether in the present or some indefinite future, are political. Jesus does not correspond to the hoped-for political messiah; politically he has no power: his is a path of suffering. (Ellis, 572)

your midst. Come and join in this movement of God's Spirit." These words of good news fed the starving spirits of the common folk.

A beatitude (11:6) If Jesus' words and actions confused John the Baptist, then they could certainly confuse the average peasant who expected a Messiah dressed in military garb and spouting violent words against Rome. In order to help the confused, Jesus ends with a beatitude. Normally, we think of the beatitudes as the beginning of the Sermon on the Mount; however, scattered throughout the New Testament are numerous blessings for those who have ears to hear and eyes to see.

Jesus' blessing is directed at those who find "no offense" in him. The New American Standard translates, "Blessed is [the one] who keeps from stumbling over me." The word "stumbling" is *skandalon*, from which we get the word "scandal." This word captures Matthew's point well. The actions and words of Jesus caused people like John to stumble, because their expectations of the Messiah were not being met. Because of preconceived ideas about the Messiah, many people did not recognize Jesus as the Messiah. Jesus prayed that all who saw his works or heard his words might be awakened to the new image of the Messiah. If they did, they were blessed.

Understanding

Advent is the best time of the season to ask the question "Who is Jesus?" Before we assume that this question has an easy answer and takes little thought, we should remember that even John the Baptist struggled with this question, and he knew the flesh-and-blood Jesus! In the last 2000 years, much gets in our way of trying to recognize Jesus as the Messiah. For example, customs practiced during this season of the year often hinder our perception of Jesus' identity. The poem "Christ Climbed Down" captures some of the elements that can distort our picture of Jesus.

Christ climbed down
from His bare Tree
this year
and ran away to where
there were no rootless Christmas trees
hung with candy canes and breakable stars.

Christ climbed down
from His bare Tree
this year
and ran away to where
no fat handshaking stranger
in a red flannel suit
and a fake white beard
went around passing himself off
as some sort of North Pole saint
crossing the desert to Bethlehem
Pennsylvania
in a Volkswagen sled
drawn by rollicking Adirondack reindeer
with German names
and bearing sacks of Humble Gifts
from Saks Fifth Avenue
for everybody's imagined Christ child.
(Johnson & Troiano, 313, 314)

Albert Schweitzer, the missionary, musician, physician, and scholar, once wrote that another way we miss the identity of Jesus is by our tendency to try to re-create Jesus in our own image (Schweitzer, 4). In other words, we have a tendency to assemble the pieces of the puzzle of Jesus in such a way that he looks and acts a lot like us. Another author puts it this way: "[Jesus] is wheeled in to give support to social or political programs of one persuasion or another, to undergird strict morality here or to offer freedom from constricting regulations there. But the question as to which Jesus we are talking about will not go away" (Wright, 10). Our own powerful experiences can sometimes allow us to construct a portrait of Jesus that is quite different from the Messiah who came to Bethlehem.

We also need to consider the humanness of Jesus, which the birth through Mary highlights. Clarence Jordan put it this way: "We create in our minds an image of [Jesus] as a superbeing, and thus safely remove him from our present experience and his insistent demands on us. We manage to keep him in his elevated and removed position by not allowing any familiarity with him or the Scriptures. Any attempt to make him human and embarrassingly present is angrily denounced as sacrilegious. By carefully preserving our image of him as God, we no longer have to deal with him as Son of Man. That is, by protecting his deity we can escape his humanity" (Lee, 186). Does the humanness of Jesus challenge our understanding of him as Messiah? Can our Messiah have dirt under his fingernails, and splinters in his hands?

? How might your portrait of Jesus need refashioning?

What About Me?

Who is Jesus? This famous question is asked by young children and scholars alike. It seems like an easy question, but the answer is strangely elusive. The description of Jesus as found in the Gospels is our foundation for understanding his identity, but even after we carefully recognize him as the Messiah, still the image changes. Jesus the Messiah is continually calling us to a deeper understanding, and perhaps a different one.

John's understanding of the coming one is corrected by learning of Jesus as the one who heals and spreads good news. In other words, while John expected one who would remove evil, Jesus came and restored the good and holy. What a shock for those like John who expected a Remover Messiah, but got a Restorer Messiah. The one who comes restores, ends any exile, and enlightens the dark night. The Messiah is one who through his actions and words is in the process of restoring. What about your image of Jesus challenges you? How does the Messiah meet your expectations? How does the Messiah surpass your expectations? Which pieces of the puzzle have fallen into place? Which ones are you still trying to make fit?

Resources

Linda McKinnish Bridges, *The Church's Portraits of Jesus*, (Macon GA, Smyth & Helwys Publishing, 1997).

J. Bradley Chance, "John the Baptist," *Mercer Dictionary of the Bible*, ed. Watson E. Mills et al. (Macon GA: Mercer University Press, 1990).

Judy Yates Ellis, "Messiah/Messianism," *Mercer Dictionary of the Bible*, ed. Watson E. Mills et al. (Macon GA: Mercer University Press, 1990).

Pegram Johnson and Edna M. Troiano, eds., *The Roads to Bethlehem* (Louisville KY: Westminster/John Knox Press, 1993).

Dallas Lee, *The Cotton Patch Evidence* (San Francisco: Harper & Row, 1971).

J. Ramsey Michaels, *Servant and Son: Jesus in Parable and Gospel* (Atlanta: John Knox Press, 1981).

J. Ramsey Michaels, "Jesus," *Mercer Dictionary of the Bible*, ed. Watson Mills et al. (Macon GA: Mercer University Press, 1990).

Albert Schweitzer, *The Quest of the Historical Jesus* (London: Adam & Charles Black, 1945).

PBS and WGBH/Frontline, "From Jesus to Christ: Synopsis of the Program," (New Content, 1998), *Frontline Online*, http://www.pbs.org/wgbh/pages/frontline/shows/religion/etc/synopsis.html, [24 April 1998].

N. T. Wright, *Jesus and the Victory of God* (Minneapolis: Fortress Press, 1996).

A PUZZLING
MESSIAH

Matthew 11:2-11

Introduction

At times, Bible study can become pretty predictable. Teachers say the right things. Students ask the right questions. Possibilities for dissent, disagreement, displeasure, or doubt—well, they are run through the dishwasher. The kitchen is always clean. At Bible study, we sometimes create a climate that smashes even a hint of "How can that be?" Or, "Sometimes I have a hard time believing, much less doing what Jesus told us to do."

The Bible is not nearly as antiseptic as some of our Bible study discussions. Moses argued with God; sometimes God had a hard time with him. The Psalms tell of people who were not shy about complaining against and arguing with God. This session's text is similar to the style of Moses and the Psalms. Last session we left John the Baptizer in the wilderness of Judea. He was the great prophet/evangelist. Thousands of people went to the wilderness to hear him. He was a popular and bold leader. Jesus comes to him, submits to his baptism and from John's stage launches his own career. Much of Jesus' early message was taken almost word-for-word from John. "The time is fulfilled, and the kingdom of God has come near; repent, and believe in the good news" (Mk 1:15).

After the baptism of Jesus everything went downhill for John. Herod Antipas, the ruler of Galilee, went to Rome to visit his brother. While there, Herod seduced his brother's wife. Herod Antipas returned to Galilee, divorced his wife and took his brother's wife. John the Baptizer publicly denounced Herod's actions. For his boldness, John was put in prison. And while John suffered in isolation, the ministry of Jesus blossomed like a spring flower.

After several months, John receives word about Jesus' work. What John expected of Jesus and what he was hearing weren't exactly the same. In fact, sometimes Jesus was very different from what he expected.

I. Did I Get it Right? 11:2-3.

This text has caught my imagination. I can see the man who pulled people all the way from Jerusalem to Jordan. Now, he is not nearly so colorful. He is in a hole in the ground (that's the way prisons were built in those days). The only light was at the top of a shaft. John was down in the bottom where it was dark. It was more than lonesome. It was enough to break anyone's spirit.

Looking back, we call John the forerunner, the prophet who announced the coming of Jesus. But John didn't have the perspective of two thousand years. From the floor of that prison he didn't have much perspective at all.

What John had been hearing about Jesus did not sound like the Messiah he had envisioned. Miracles were fine, but where was the promised kingdom? When were the Romans going to go home? Why was Jesus so caught up in helping and healing? When was he going to set up a throne in Jerusalem? The text does not say John thought these thoughts. I am trying to think as John might have thought.

John was human and humans doubt. Is it reasonable to assume that John doubted for reasons such as these:

(1) He was isolated. I try to be an inner-directed person, but I draw much support from the people around me. When I am with God's people, I tend to be godly. They support and encourage right thinking and right conduct. Isolation is hard. This is why absence from church can injure the soul. Isolation is a breeding place for doubt.

(2) He was at risk. The danger of death can dampen the most positive spirit. What would happen to him? If he was going to die, when and how? In this climate, doubt grows like a wicked fungus.

(3) He was a child of the Old Testament and of Jewish thinking about the Messiah. John was a prophet, but Jewish expectations about Jesus were well formed. A problem for friends and enemies of Jesus throughout his ministry, Jesus was not acting like he was supposed to.

Put all these things together, and out of them can come serious doubt. John probably repeatedly asked himself, "Did I do the right thing?"

I've been in some scrapes and scuffles in my life. Reflecting on them, I sometimes wonder, "Did I do the right thing?" I think of other ways I might have spoken, or acted. Did I make a mistake? Did I misread the word from the Lord? If I think these thoughts, is it unreasonable to think John might have had them too? Doubt is not a sin, but doubt left untended can become sin.

II. An Answer not an Argument, 11:4-6.

John the Baptizer had disciples and some of them did not desert him. During one of their visits, John told them to go to Jesus to ask, "Are you the one who is to come, or are we to wait for another?" (Mt 11:3).

This question is not coming from a timid soul, it is coming from the boldest spokesperson for God in his time. People followed John and no doubt, he still had much influence. Jesus would not brush aside a question from John. Their special relationship required a serious answer. There are three things in Jesus' response:

(1) He did not scold John for doubting. This is encouraging. All people have down times. In down times, doubt creeps in like weeds in a garden. If Jesus did not put John down for his doubt, maybe he won't put us down either. This is a hopeful word.

(2) Jesus did not give John a carefully reasoned argument about the nature of the Kingdom of God and Messiah. The text offers no theology. "Go and tell John what you hear and see: the blind receive their sight, the lame walk, the lepers are cleansed, the deaf hear, the dead are raised, and the poor have good news brought to them" (11:4-5). Both John and Jesus knew the Old Testament. It was from the Old Testament they found their guideline for what the Messiah would be.

Here are three quotations from Isaiah:

• "On that day the deaf shall hear the words of a scroll,.. the eyes of the blind shall see. The meek shall obtain fresh joy in the Lord, and the neediest people shall exult in the Holy One of Israel" (Isa 29:18-19).

• "Then the eyes of the blind shall be opened, and the ears of the deaf unstopped; then the lame shall leap like a deer, and the tongue of the speechless sing for joy. For waters shall break forth in the wilderness, and streams in the desert" (Isa 5:5-6).

• "The spirit of the Lord God is upon me, because the Lord has anointed me; he has sent me to bring good news to the oppressed, to bind up the brokenhearted, to proclaim liberty to the captives, and release to the prisoners; to proclaim the year of the Lord's favor...To comfort all who mourn" (Isa 61:1-2).

Jesus' words to John are a loose translation of Isaiah. Jesus was a living fulfillment of all Isaiah said the Messiah would be. These words would not have been lost on John.

(3) Then Jesus concluded this way: "And blessed is anyone who takes no offense at me" (11:6). Often God does not act as we think God will or even should act. Who would ever have guessed God would come as a baby in a stable? Who would have imagined that the Messiah would go to the cross? All the gospels record times when it is obvious that neither disciples nor critics were satisfied with how Jesus projected himself. When our expectations of what God should do become too rigid, we can't recognize God. God gets to be God. We are the ones who must adjust, enlarge, shift, and rethink.

III. The Man Jesus Praised, 11:7-11.

Jesus accurately reflects God's standards. Jesus praised John the Baptizer.

(1) John was not a crowd-pleaser. Jesus put it this way: "What did you go out into the wilderness to look at? A reed shaken by the wind?" (Mt 11:7b). A reed was a pliable water plant that would sway in the least breeze. John was not "a reed shaken by the wind." He was a courageous person of deep convictions. He was not afraid of Pharisees and Sadducees. He was not afraid to tell Herod Antipas he had sinned. John was a profile of a prophet,

and Jesus praised his moral strength. Jesus would like to see the same moral strength in us.

(2) John did not run with the comfortable crowd. "What then did you go out to see? Someone dressed in soft robes? Look, those who wear soft robes are in royal palaces" (Mt 11:8). Throughout the New Testament runs a prejudice against currying the favor of the rich. Paul wrote to Corinth saying, "not many of you were wise,...Not many were powerful,...Not many were of noble birth" (1 Cor 1:26). The Epistle of James continues the same theme against the rich (Jas 5:1-6). Comfortable clergy people have been the curse of good religion since the Old Testament. John would have no part of the comfortable set.

(3) Jesus called John a prophet. "See, I am sending my messenger ahead of you, who will prepare your way before you" (11:10). He quoted from Malachi 3:1. John met scriptural standards for a prophet. We don't usually think of ourselves as prophets. Such is the stuff of heroes, and we see ourselves as "just folks." But every age needs a few prophets. There may be a touch of the prophet in us if only we would let it out.

John the Baptizer had the spiritual sensitivity to recognize Jesus as the Messiah. He baptized him. But later when life closed in, his insight was not as clear. Confusion and puzzlement overwhelmed the sure eye of the prophet. That's my story. Sometimes I've read the culture and declared the intention of God. I've spoken for God and gotten it right. But later, I've lost my way. This text is hope and heart for all of us sometime prophets who fall into doubt. Take heart.

Notes

Notes

4

FOLLOWING THE RIGHTEOUS
SPIRIT OF CHRISTMAS

Matthew 1:18-25

Central Questions

• How have you experienced God's presence?
• When have you witnessed righteousness that went beyond
  expectations?
• When do traditions and expectations get in the way of the kind
  of righteousness to which Jesus calls us?

Scripture

Matthew 1:18-25 Now the birth of Jesus the Messiah took place
in this way. When his mother Mary had been engaged to Joseph,
but before they lived together, she was found to be with child
from the Holy Spirit. 19 Her husband Joseph, being a righteous
man and unwilling to expose her to public disgrace, planned to
dismiss her quietly. 20 But just when he had resolved to do this,
an angel of the Lord appeared to him in a dream and said,
"Joseph, son of David, do not be afraid to take Mary as your wife,
for the child conceived in her is from the Holy Spirit. 21 She will
bear a son, and you are to name him Jesus, for he will save his
people from their sins." 22 All this took place to fulfill what had
been spoken by the Lord through the prophet: 23 "Look, the
virgin shall conceive and bear a son, and they shall name him
Emmanuel," which means, "God is with us." 24 When Joseph
awoke from sleep, he did as the angel of the Lord commanded
him; he took her as his wife, 25 but had no marital relations with
her until she had borne a son; and he named him Jesus.

Remembering

Although the Sunday of Advent, the Sunday immediately prior to Christmas, is one of the most joyful in all the Christian year, it can also be one of the most difficult when it comes to studying a lesson. It's difficult because we know the Christmas story so well, we cannot imagine anything new being added. Usually, however, we read the familiar story of Matthew 1:18-25 without paying much attention to the details. Knowing the story so well, we also recall Luke's account of Jesus' birth (Lk 2:1-20) and miss the unique themes found in Matthew. In addition, we may bring traditions from carols and partially remembered Christmas pageants into our reading of the Christmas story.

A careful and detailed reading of Matthew 1:18-25, however, reveals unique themes that the author has reserved especially for a close reading. In such a reading, we may be surprised to discover that, though the birth of Jesus forms the heart of this story, we are also asked to consider how God's will is revealed to us and how we will respond to this revelation.

Studying

In all the Christmas programs performed this season, a great amount of time and effort goes into the practicing of parts. Usually, everyone is given a few lines to recite so that no one is left out of the drama of Christmas. Yet if Matthew 1:18-25 were the only script used, only two speakers would be necessary: the narrator and the angel. Indeed, the only action Matthew portrays is Joseph's act at the very end of the story: "He [Joseph] took her as his wife" (1:24). With these hints in the story of Jesus' birth, Matthew directs our attention to some details of great importance.

The crisis verging on tragedy (1:18-19) The narrator very briefly (in the space of two verses) reveals the characters and situation. Mary was engaged to Joseph, and this formal custom is good news. She was also pregnant, however, and this crisis could easily turn into a tragedy. Engagement or betrothal in the first century is not like engagement in twentieth-century America. It is the "initial phrase of the marriage process in which prospective spouses were set apart for each other. Though a betrothed couple did not live together, a formal divorce was required to break the public establishment of the betrothal" (Pilch, 10).

Marriage in the first century was not based upon romanticized love that populates the pages of novels or television shows today. Marriages such as that of Mary and Joseph were typically arranged by parents. Two families would unite through the marriage of their children primarily in order to secure or advance either their financial circumstances or their social positions or both. Therefore, Mary's pregnancy was not one that affected her only, but in a very real sense, her entire village! Though the men of the village, including Joseph, would not immediately have known about Mary's pregnancy, the village women "would have noticed that she was not partici-pating in their obligatory monthly ritual purification" (Pilch, 11). The narrator, however, wants the reader to know in advance that Mary's was no ordinary preg-nancy. Mary was "with child from the Holy Spirit" (1:18).

> In Old Testament days, the marriage process was initiated by the groom's father. Negotiations between families were followed by the presentation of gifts or a payment called the *mohar*. Then began the customary betrothal. The woman was then considered a wife, but consummation of the marriage came later. (Joines, 554)

If the people of the village had learned that Mary was pregnant, they undoubtedly would have assumed the expected child to be the result of an illicit affair, not the result of the Holy Spirit. Mary knew the inevitable consequences of being judged guilty of an unlawful liaison. According to Jewish law, two options were possible: she could have been taken to a priest for a curse to be uttered over her to render her childless (Num 4:11-28), or she could have been stoned (Deut 22:13-21).

Joseph prevented the crisis from becoming a tragedy. The narrator carefully describes him as a righteous person. Righteousness, following the will of God, is a theme running throughout Matthew. According to ancient Jews, following the Law is considered righteous. The Law reveals the will of God. It gives direction for everyday life and its dilemmas. Joseph was facing a dilemma, but remarkably, he does not follow the letter of the Law. As one scholar has put it, "Joseph, contrary to the behavior expected of one who is [righteous], has already decided not to go by the letter of the law, but chose out of consideration for Mary to divorce her quietly" (Boring, 134). Following the letter of the law for Mary's situation might very well have ended her life.

A dream, an angel, a revelation (1:20-23) Joseph's dream adds an extra dimension to our understanding of revelation and righteous actions. Joseph's revelatory dream was instructive. It revealed the purpose of the one soon to be born. The child was to be a son, and he would "save his people from their sins" (1:21). Sin in Matthew's understanding means "an evil will and intention expressed in violating the divine will" (Carter, 124). The dream also revealed the child's name, Emmanuel. This name describes Jesus' character and expresses the gift of God's presence. Jesus will be present with us. Jesus' presence with us forms a bookend for the entire Gospel of Matthew. Jesus' name is disclosed in Chapter 1 as "God with us." In the last chapter of Matthew, Jesus lets the disciples know that Emmanuel is still his name and purpose when he declares, "I am with you always" (28:20).

> In the New Testament, persons are considered righteous if they conform to the prevailing legal and moral system of society. Righteousness is both the standard to which one conforms and one's status with respect to society. Beyond the legal obligation, however, is the moral obligation. Persons who possess certain qualities that contribute to the moral fiber of society are considered righteous. Righteousness is a virtue, the mark of a productive member of society. (Sheeley, 765).

Obedience (1:24,25) When Joseph wakes from his dream, he knows more about Mary's situation and the child. God's will has been revealed to him. Joseph has already gone beyond the letter of law by agreeing to divorce Mary quietly. What would Joseph do now that he knew the child within Mary to be from God? If Jesus were to be of Davidic lineage, it would only happen through Joseph's adoption of him. Would he have the righteousness that exceeded expectations? In verses 18-25, only one action is recorded: Joseph "took her to be his wife." Joseph is the first to demonstrate the righteousness of the Kingdom of God.

Too often we skip over the implications of this single action in verses 18-25: Joseph took Mary as his wife. Joseph married Mary even though the people of the village would not have understood it. Some perhaps already thought him soft regarding the Law in his intention to divorce Mary quietly. What would they think and say about his marrying her? It is doubtful that claiming her child was of the Holy Spirit would have made much of an impression on the village folk. Such a claim would likely have provoked laughter and derision upon Joseph for believing such a tale. Yet Joseph's actions were righteous because he was obedient to the revelation from God.

Understanding

Many people think that being "religiously correct" means living according to church folks' expectations. Joseph could have been religiously correct, but he listened to God, and his actions went beyond established expectations. Are there times when we need to step out and away from the traditional expectation because of a greater righteousness?

Joseph's reaction to Mary's conception challenges our response to the continuing revelation of the good news in Scripture. We often take the Scriptures for granted. The Scriptures can reveal to us the greater righteousness exemplified in the birth, life, and death of Jesus, inspiring us to righteous action.

We also too quickly discount revelatory experiences. Our experiences with fellow believers can be a part of God's continuing revelation. Perhaps even our dreams can reveal truth from God. One of my friends shared his dream after the death of a colleague. In the dream, he found himself in a large auditorium waiting for the funeral of our departed colleague. As in many dreams, the circumstances and sequence of events in his dream defied ordinary logic. Much to his surprise, in the midst of all the people, he recognized another colleague who had died several years earlier. With surprise and shock, my friend tried to ask how he could be there and what he was doing. His former colleague smiled and said, "I just came to say that Hugh is fine. I thought you might like to know that. Let everybody know, would you? He's fine now." Not all dreams are revelatory, and some people might question the significance of my colleague's dream. Still, to believe that God cannot continue to use dreams to speak to modern people is to limit an infinite God.

When have you stepped outside traditional expectation because of a greater righteousness??

What About Me?

The movie *Amistad*, which first appeared in movie theaters in 1997, is the true story of forty-four Africans taken as slaves who, through a series of tragic circumstances, wind up in a prison in America. They were imprisoned, awaiting an eventual trial before Supreme Court justices who would decide if they could be freed to return home to Africa. One of them receives a Bible. Day after day the captive African looks at the pages. One day while staring at the Bible pages, another imprisoned African challenges him: "You aren't fooling anyone. I know you can't read those words." The holder of the book acknowledges that he cannot read it; nevertheless, he believes he understands the story and shows the beautiful engravings scattered throughout the Bible depicting the life of Jesus. He points his finger at a picture of the newborn baby Jesus with Mary and Joseph, looks up at his companion, and says, "Even though I don't understand what it says, I do know that from this point on everything changes."

With the birth of Jesus everything *does* change. Righteousness has a new standard, set by Jesus. We must be open to the revelation that God continues to give us through Scripture and other means. Perhaps the biggest challenge is to be obedient to God, achieving the new righteousness ushered in by the birth of the child Jesus. Will we follow the righteousness of Jesus?

Resources

Warren Carter, Matthew: Storyteller, *Interpreter, Evangelist* (Peabody MA: Hendrickson, 1997).

Roberston Davies, *The Merry Heart* (New York: Viking, 1997).

Kerri Howell et al., "What Causes Dreams?" *American Institute for Learning* (AIL), http://www.ail.org/Media/Dreams/VisualDreams/causes/causes.html (30 April 1998).

Karen Randolph Joines, "Marriage in the Old Testament," *Mercer Dictionary of the Bible*, ed. Watson E. Mill et al. (Macon GA: Mercer University Press, 1990).

David L. Mueller, "Concept of Revelation," *Mercer Dictionary of the Bible*, ed. Watson E. Mill et al. (Macon GA: Mercer University Press, 1990).

John J. Pilch, *The Cultural World of Jesus: Sunday by Sunday*, Cycle A (Collegeville MN: The Liturgical Press, 1995).

Steven M. Sheeley, "Righteousness in the New Testament," *Mercer Dictionary of the Bible*, ed. Watson E. Mills et al. (Macon GA: Mercer University Press, 1990).

Joseph L. Trafton, "Joseph," *Mercer Dictionary of the Bible*, ed. Watson E. Mills et al. (Macon GA: Mercer University Press, 1990).

FOLLOWING THE RIGHTEOUS SPIRIT OF CHRISTMAS

Matthew 1:18-25

Introduction

Joseph is the unsung hero in the Christmas story. Joseph is mentioned only three times in Luke's account of Jesus' birth (1:27; 2:4; 2:16). Matthew, however, writes a paragraph. Our lesson is taken from that paragraph.

Some knowledge of Jewish culture will help our understanding of this text.

(1) "Engaged" (1:18). Marriages were arranged. An engagement was a year-long period during which the couple did not live together *but* they were considered legally married. To break an "engagement" required a divorce. Unfaithfulness during the year of engagement was considered adultery.

(2) Joseph was called "a righteous man" (1:19a). This means he was making a serious attempt to live his life according to the Law of Moses. His religion was important to him.

(3) "Unwilling to expose her to public disgrace, planned to dismiss her quietly" (1:19b). If Joseph went by the letter of the law, he had justification to have Mary put to death (Deut 22:23-27). This custom had softened by the time of Jesus. Offending women were not put to death. According to first century practice, Joseph could have divorced Mary and she would have become a public example of immorality. The social ostracizing would have been brutal. Joseph did not want this for Mary, but neither was he willing to overlook her unfaithfulness. He wanted to deal with her as gently as law and custom would allow.

One more peculiarity lies buried in this text. We read this story in the light of Luke. You know from the start that "the angel Gabriel was sent by God to...a virgin engaged to a man whose name was Joseph" (Lk 1:26-27). Matthew's readers do not know this and will not know it until Matthew's gospel and Luke's gospel are bound together in a cluster of "approved books" for the church (officially not until 367 AD). According to Matthew's account, Joseph did not know an angel had visited Mary. He did not know how she got pregnant. This perspective will add suspense to our story and it can enhance our appreciation for Joseph.

I. Discover: What Do I Do?, 1:18-19.

We have a hard time understanding Joseph's situation. We don't know how well he knew Mary or if he had ever seen her. But we do know that one day a jolting piece of news came to Joseph. The woman to whom he was engaged was pregnant. How she got pregnant, and by whom, he did not know. Matthew inserts into the text an explanation for the reader: "from the Holy Spirit" (1:18b). But that would bring no peace to Joseph.

Two conflicting factors need to be taken into account when considering Joseph's predicament:

(1) Moses was "a righteous man." The Law was Joseph's guideline. As a first century "righteous man," he should condemn Mary.

(2) Joseph did not do what was expected. He is "a righteous man," *and* he cares for Mary. He was "unwilling to expose her to public disgrace" (1:19b). So, he set the strict interpretation of the law aside and opted for the most merciful course open to him. He "planned to dismiss her quietly" (1:19c).

Law and grace are pulling against each other in the conscience of a good man. Joseph did two things:

(1) He did the most merciful thing a devout Jew could do. He did not want to hurt Mary.

(2) He was not willing to "let bygones be bygones." Mary's actions are serious and he will not go on with the marriage.

This would have been a middle course for "a righteous man." Was he strictly obeying the law? No. Was he letting her off? No. He was looking for law with grace. This would not have been a comfortable choice for "a righteous man." Today, we have plenty of people willing to be "righteous." And their interpretation of the law is strict and hard. We have another group of people who are willing to disregard the law altogether; go ahead and marry her. Everybody makes mistakes. Joseph's course has something to teach us.

II. Dream: Touched by an Angel, 1:20-21.

Three times during the infancy of Jesus, God spoke to Joseph through a dream (1:20-21; 2:13; 2:19-20). Prophets did not deliver this word, it was delivered by an angel in a dream. The first of Joseph's dreams from God brings amazing news.

(1) "Do not be afraid to take Mary as your wife" (1:20b). This meant, "Go ahead and marry Mary. Do not back out of the 'engagement.'"

(2) "The child conceived in her is from the Holy Spirit" (1:20c). Now Joseph knows what Mary knows.

(3) "You are to name him Jesus, for he will save his people from their sins" (1:21). *The New Interpreter's Bible* has this observation about the name Jesus: "These are all forms of the English name, Joshua...This Joshua...Jesus was the successor to Moses' authority" (*The New Interpreter's Bible*, Vol. VIII, Nashville: Abingdon Press, 1995, 134). The first Joshua succeeded Moses, so a second Joshua would succeed Moses as spiritual guide to God's people. We have no way of knowing how much of this Joseph understood. "He will save his people from their sins" must have seemed farfetched. But Joseph did not doubt; he believed the angel.

III. Discourses: Personal Life Has Been Eclipsed by Larger Plans, 1:22-23.

With these verses, Matthew interrupts the story to offer an interpretation. "All this took place to fulfill..." (1:22a). Matthew is writing for a Jewish audience, but not so much to persuade outsiders to believe in Jesus. Matthew was trying to help Jewish Christians understand continuity. Did Jesus break with Moses and Elijah? Matthew says "No". Are Jews still the people of God? Matthew struggles with this question. Who is Jesus in relation to Old Testament history? Three ideas come from verses 22-23:

(1) *Continuity.* Jesus is not a newcomer to the Jews. Jesus is the fulfillment of prophesy. He is a part of all God intends for Jews. "All this took place to fulfill what had been spoken by the Lord through the prophet: Look, the virgin shall conceive and bear a son..." (1:22-23a). Matthew quotes from Isaiah 7:14. Matthew shows that Jesus is not from outside Judaism; he is from deep within their history. This is not change; this is continuity. God is still working through Jews to "save his people from their sins." There is development in what God is doing, but God has not made radical change.

(2) *Fulfillment.* Prophecies of hundreds of years are coming to pass. God had a design and Jesus is its fulfillment. So, Isaiah's prophecy, once understood in a limited way (Judah will be delivered from war) is now understood on a grand scale. Judah will be delivered from all that separates it from God. In Christ, God fulfills all that the prophets promised. This is a recurring theme in Matthew.

(3) *Emmanuel.* Jesus will be named "God with us," the word's literal meaning. By Matthew's estimate, God came nearer in Jesus than God had ever come before. The other gospels support Matthew's claim. John tells of Jesus' answering Philip's question: "Lord, show us the Father..." And Jesus replies, "Whoever has seen me has seen the Father" (Jn 14:8-9). "God with us" was lived out before them. God came near.

So the message John the Baptizer spoke, "Repent, for the kingdom of heaven has come near" (3:2), was more than a figure of speech. It was fleshed out in Emmanuel, who was and remains "God with us."

After an interpretation of who Jesus was in relation to Old Testament prophecy, Matthew continues the story. It is almost as if he put a parenthesis in the text (verses 1:22-23).

IV. Decision: Obedience and Faith Are the Legacy of a Good Man, 1:24-25.

Joseph awoke from his dream. We don't know if he pondered what the angel said. In a display of faith unlike any in Scripture, we are told what Joseph did.

(1) "He took her (Mary) as his wife" (1:24b). He would not divorce her, he would marry her. And what of embarrassment? What if the women of the town "talked"? What if the men made snide remarks? We are not given a hint of how that was handled. There had to be difficult moments in dealing with the results of his decision. Pregnancy is not hidden in a small town.

(2) He postponed sex with his wife "until she had borne a son" (1:25a). He did nothing to interfere with God's plan. Whatever a groom's expectation in that culture, that expectation was denied until God's purpose in Mary's baby came to fulfillment. One more detail: Matthew is making sure we know that Joseph was not the father of Mary's baby.

(3) "He named him Jesus" (1:25b). Naming the child was of more consequence to a first-century Jew than it is to us today. "By naming the child, he effectively adopts Jesus into the Davidic line. Matthew, and the Bible generally, invests great power in declarations and naming. Being named by Joseph, Jesus becomes part of the Davidic line" (*The New Interpreter's Bible*, Vol. VIII, 135). The early Church often associated Jesus with the lineage of David. Jesus could be so connected because Joseph did what the angel asked him to do.

Obedience and faith describe Joseph. The Bible does not hold one word that Joseph said, but Joseph's place is still significant. He had faith to believe God's angel. He obeyed God. In the larger scheme of things, Joseph was a minor figure, but for a moment he was center stage. He played his part well. The gospels tell us more of Mary than Joseph. He must have died before Jesus began his ministry. He is not mentioned in any of the family appearances in Jesus' ministry. But just off-stage, there was a man who believed incredible things...that Mary's baby was of the Holy Spirit...that God wanted him to act as the earthly father for God's Son...that God wanted him to keep and help a woman who was helpless in the culture of her time. Maybe Joseph wasn't such a bit player after all.

Notes

Notes

WHEN KINGDOMS COLLIDE

Matthew 2:13-23

Central Questions

• How do you recognize the providence of God?
• How do we express our assurance in God's providence in a violent world?
• What can you do to help your community more closely resemble the Kingdom of God?

Scripture

Matthew 2:13-23 Now after they had left, an angel of the Lord appeared to Joseph in a dream and said, "Get up, take the child and his mother, and flee to Egypt, and remain there until I tell you; for Herod is about to search for the child, to destroy him." 14 Then Joseph got up, took the child and his mother by night, and went to Egypt, 15 and remained there until the death of Herod. This was to fulfill what had been spoken by the Lord through the prophet, "Out of Egypt I have called my son." 16 When Herod saw that he had been tricked by the wise men, he was infuriated, and he sent and killed all the children in and around Bethlehem who were two years old or under, according to the time that he had learned from the wise men. 17 Then was fulfilled what had been spoken through the prophet Jeremiah: 18 "A voice was heard in Ramah, wailing and loud lamentation, Rachel weeping for her children; she refused to be consoled, because they are no more." 19 When Herod died, an angel of the Lord suddenly appeared in a dream to Joseph in Egypt and said, 20 "Get up, take the child and his mother, and go to the land of

Israel, for those who were seeking the child's life are dead."
21 Then Joseph got up, took the child and his mother, and went
to the land of Israel. 22 But when he heard that Archelaus was
ruling over Judea in place of his father Herod, he was afraid to go
there. And after being warned in a dream, he went away to the
district of Galilee. 23 There he made his home in a town called
Nazareth, so that what had been spoken through the prophets
might be fulfilled, "He will be called a Nazorean."

Remembering

Christmas is over, and now we have to clean up. Some of us have
already started putting away the signs of Christmas. The orna-
ments are carefully tucked into their designated boxes. By
incredible feats of engineering, the tree is folded and stuffed back
into its original box. Baby Jesus, Mary, Joseph, and the rest of the
Nativity cast are already assigned to their proper boxes and cush-
ioned with tissue paper to await another year. The carols and
Christmas songs are no longer playing. Christmas is over, and we
move on. The holiday was nice, but the next is quickly approach-
ing, and we have much to do.

For Mary and Joseph, the aftermath of Jesus' coming was not as
simple as putting everything back into its place and resuming the
normal rituals of life. There was barely time to celebrate this
special event before death began to stalk them and their baby.
Death decreed by Herod the Great loomed like an ominous
shadow over this obscure peasant family. Violence was in the air.
Before long, blood would flow in the streets of Bethlehem.
Would the blood of baby Jesus be mingled with it? The Christmas
story does not end with the happy account of the birth of the
Messiah.

Before we put away Christmas and its story, perhaps we need a
reminder that the birth of Jesus was only the beginning. The
birth had immediate effects on Mary and Joseph and deadly
consequences for the entire town of Bethlehem. It meant life-and-
death decisions. It meant flight and fear, trust and providence.

The birth of Jesus is not an event to be tucked away into storage. Pondering the birth of Christ can move us to face the world with a greater awareness of God's love and presence in it. Likewise, the ruthless events surrounding the birth of Jesus can help us to reflect on God's providence in this age of violence.

Studying

On the road to Egypt (2:13-15) Matthew's account of Jesus' birth has been relatively good news to this point. The rocky beginning of Joseph and Mary's betrothal was overcome. Jesus was born without incident. This healthy birth is especially good news in an age when women often died in childbirth and newborns frequently lived only a short time. The star gazers from the East bestowed upon Jesus honor and recognition, and they presented gifts of gold, frankincense, and myrrh. The story of Jesus' birth would have a happy ending if it concluded with the giving of gifts. But Matthew records the rest of the story.

Joseph's ever present dreams shattered any illusion about life getting back to normal. Just as God's revelation had previously directed Joseph to marry (1:20), another revelation now instructed Joseph to flee with his family to Egypt because Herod the Great was seeking to kill the child. A righteous person, Joseph obeyed that very night.

Herod's reputation of at least 30 years only confirmed the truth of the angel's words. Herod was a great builder, a great military leader, and a great friend to Rome. He was also a great schemer, a great oppressor, and a great paranoid. The fortresses around the country were testimony to his insecurity. The executions of spouses and sons were testimony to his punitive and merciless instability. If he refused to spare his own sons for fear that they craved his title as King of the Judeans, then he certainly would not allow anyone else—even a baby—to endanger his position.

Joseph fled with Mary and the baby to Egypt. People of that day often fled to Egypt to evade Herod's reach. Besides a place of refuge, Egypt was also the land of Moses. Reading the story of Jesus' birth and early trials in the Gospel of Matthew, we hear echoes from the life of Moses. As an infant, Moses was pursued by a ruler who wanted his death. Moses was miraculously saved from death and came out of Egypt to free his people. Moses, the ideal leader-liberator, is the model for Matthew's portrayal of Jesus' life in his Gospel. Jesus is like the great liberator Moses, but Jesus' words and deeds greatly surpass those of Moses.

Violence and the Kingdom (2:16-18) Verses 16-18 record what has traditionally been called the Slaughter of the Innocents. As we celebrate the miracle of Jesus' safety, we should not casually overlook the pain felt by the village of Bethlehem.

The number of male children killed in Bethlehem on Herod's orders is unknown. Bethlehem was a small village of only about a hundred people (Pilch, 14). The children put to the sword probably numbered in the upper teens, yet the wailing raised on that day must have echoed with the voices of every person in Bethlehem. For who could refrain from crying as children screaming "mother" and "father" reached out with tiny fingers toward confused and restrained parents.

> In some traditions, the sad event of Herod's killing of Bethlehem children two years old and under is commemorated on December 28, called Childermas or the Feast of Holy Innocents' Day.

Although this massacre in Bethlehem was characteristic of Herod's notorious paranoia and methods, no sources apart from the account in Matthew record the tragedy. These few deaths in a small village would not have been sufficiently significant in the eyes of ancient historians to rate putting quill to papyrus in order to record them.

The writer of Revelation, however, saw Herod's attempt to kill Jesus as more than a blip on the time line of history. Writing in a far different style than Matthew, John depicts this event as Death coming to hunt Jesus. In Revelation 12:4b-5, John records these words: "Then the dragon stood before the woman who was about to bear a child, so that he might devour her child as soon as it was born. And she gave birth to a son, a male child, who is to rule all the nations with a rod of iron. But her child was snatched away and taken to God and to his throne." For John, this was not some insignificant event. He understood Jesus' birth and miraculous saving to have universal significance.

Matthew does not use the bold and symbolic language of John to illustrate the significance of the Messiah's coming and the trials associated with it. He did, however, use Old Testament prophecy to remind the reader of God's plan. He points to the events happening in Jesus' life as the fulfillment of Scripture. As one writer states, "Matthew's mind and text are thoroughly steeped in the Scriptures, containing considerably more such quotations and allusions than any of the other Gospels" (Boring, 151).

Fleeing from Bethlehem, living in Egypt, and finally settling in Nazareth is Matthew's way of communicating that God was active in every moment of Jesus' life. The use of Old Testament prophecy to proclaim God's actions illustrates that Jesus' birth had always been part of God's initiative to liberate humanity from exile. Jesus is the Messiah who will bring the plan to full bloom.

On the road to Nazareth (2:19-23)
Matthew ends his account of Jesus' birth and childhood where he began, with a dream. This time, Joseph's revelatory dream directs him to go back to Israel. Obediently Joseph returns, only to discover that Archelaus, son of Herod the Great, and a chip off the old block, was ruling in Judea. So, in order to put

> This suffering and distress may have been envisioned by Jeremiah when he said "Rachel is weeping for her children...because they are no more." Jeremiah 31:15b

distance between the child Jesus and this ruthless ruler of Judea, Joseph took his family to Galilee. This area was governed by Herod Antipas, whose path Jesus would cross later. In Galilee, by divine direction, they go to the city of Nazareth. The Advent road ends at this point. The road that leads from Nazareth to Jerusalem is the road of Lent and Easter.

Understanding

In Matthew's Gospel, the Kingdom of God and the kingdom of Herod collide. The kingdom of Herod was steeped in violence and oppression. Herod's oppressive administration wielded a double-edged sword of fear and repression over the people. In contrast, Jesus' birth initiated the peaceable Kingdom. It is significant that Mary, Joseph, and the child flee from Herod. They neither stop to fight nor wait for intervening angels to protect the Messiah. They flee at God's command. The Kingdom of which Jesus is the Prince is not one of violence. Citizens of God's Kingdom do not seek retaliation and revenge, but overcome evil with good (5:44; see also Rom 12:21; 1 Thess 5:15; 1 Pet 3:9, 11).

Our day may especially seem vulnerable to individuals like Herod who use their power to violate, mistreat, and destroy others. The violence is found not only in physical acts of cruelty and persecution, but also in words and attitudes. Those who follow Jesus can at times seem out of step, even deluded. Announcing to the people of Bethlehem that the Kingdom of God was supreme and that Herod's power amounted to nothing would have seemed ludicrous to parents washing blood from the streets. So, we are all confronted with a challenging question: Is it possible in overwhelming situations to trust in the providence of God? From our limited situation and our immediate struggle to be citizens of the Kingdom, the Kingdom of God may seem to have little power to help and heal when kingdoms collide.

The skeletal remains of Herod's kingdom are scattered among the museums of the world and under the shifting sand of Israel. Yet the Kingdom of God that seemed so vulnerable is found within every gathering of Christians and in our love for one another, and it is demonstrated when we follow Jesus' teaching to renounce violence (5:38-48).

What About Me?

We are called to live as citizens of the new kingdom ushered in by Jesus' birth. As a result, our priorities and values will inevitably clash with the priorities and values of other "kingdoms." What aspects of our faith distinctively set us apart as the people of God? In what ways can we express our opposition to the world's standards and values and yet not be violent in actions or words?

> When have you found it difficult to trust in God's providence?

This lesson is also a challenge for us to express our faith in very tangible ways to those who are displaced. We may be the providence of God for these people and the lifeline that sustains and empowers them to reach the potential God has in store for them. With the uncertainty of careers, jobs, health, marriages, parenting, and many other aspects of life, we are all displaced at some point. We need each other. Let us live our faith in such a way that we are effective conduits of God's providence and grace.

Resource

M. Eugene Boring, "Matthew," *The New Interpreter's Bible*, vol. 8 (Nashville: Abingdon Press, 1995).

Pegram Johnson and Edna M. Troiano, *The Roads from Bethlehem* (Louisville KY: Westminster/John Knox Press, 1993).

John C. H. Laughlin, "Herod," *Mercer Dictionary of the Bible*, ed. Watson Mills et al. (Macon GA: Mercer University Press, 1990).

John J. Pilch, *The Cultural World of Jesus: Sunday by Sunday*, Cycle A (Collegeville MN: The Liturgical Press, 1995).

WHEN KINGDOMS COLLIDE

Matthew 2:13-23

Introduction

Most church people think they know everything there is to know about "the Christmas story." Compared to other parts of the Bible, most church people probably do know more about the Christmas stories than they know about the Hebrews' deliverance from Egypt or Paul's journeys. Still, there are bits and pieces to "the Christmas story" that are slightly known. This session's text is material that we don't talk about much.

Telling this story will be more important than usual because it is a difficult text. Matthew was writing to Jewish Christians, making a case for Jesus having been the promised Messiah. What Matthew was trying to tell his first readers is not easy for us to hear. The way he used the Old Testament is puzzling to us. These are only some of the difficult issues in this lesson.

I. The Story.

Matthew's account of Jesus' birth is very different from Luke's. To "get into" Matthew, it would be wise not to read Luke at all, because it is so easy to combine the two accounts to make a blended nativity. We do better when we let Matthew tell his story without concern for how well it "fits" Luke. The same would apply to Luke. Matthew's sequence is as follows:

(1) The genealogy of Jesus is from Abraham to Joseph (1:1-16).

(2) Joseph is told of the unusual circumstances surrounding Mary's pregnancy (1:18-25). Mary is hardly mentioned. Joseph is the principal parent in Matthew's account. Joseph named Jesus, and in Matthew that was critical.

(3) Wise Men come "'from the East...' asking, 'Where is the child who has been born king of the Jews?'" (1:1-2). Note that Jesus is recognized by Gentiles.

(4) Joseph, Mary, and the baby Jesus are in Bethlehem. In another dream, God warns Joseph to "take the child and his mother, and flee to Egypt, and remain there until I tell you" (2:13-15). Joseph acts promptly. Like many other Jews, the family escapes Herod and finds refuge in Egypt.

(5) Herod the Great was cruel. The Romans trusted him, and he served the Romans faithfully. It would be hard to overstate his capacity for raw meanness. William Barclay illustrated Herod's murdering ways with this sad litany:

He murdered his wife Mariamne and her mother Alexandra. His eldest son, Antipater, and two other sons, Alexander and Aristobulus, were assassinated by him. Augustus, the Roman Emperor, had said bitterly that it was safer to be Herod's pig than Herod's son (Barclay, *The Gospel of Matthew*, Vol. 1, Philadelphia: Westminster Press, 1958, 20).

So, if Wise Men from the East said Jesus might rival Herod as "king of the Jews," then the baby boy must be killed. But God warned and Joseph obeyed. The infant Jesus was saved.

(6) Herod's fear of a rival had to find outlet. He calculated how to kill Jesus and determined that every male child in Bethlehem had to die. By this method, he could not miss killing the newborn "king of the Jews." This led to "the murder of the innocents" (2:16-18). Some commentators believe this is not a historical event, that it didn't really happen, because Matthew's gospel is the only account of it. It was, however, in character for Herod.

(7) Because of Joseph's alert obedience, Mary and Jesus are safe in Egypt.

(8) Finally, Herod the Great dies. At his death, God spoke a third time to Joseph in a dream. "Get up, take the child and his mother, and go to the land of Israel, for those who were seeking the child's life are dead" (2:20). Always obedient to God's voice, Joseph went back to Israel.

(9) Joseph was prudent. Archelaus, son of Herod the Great, was the new ruler over Judea. Like his father, he was unpredictable

and often murderous. Joseph did not go back to Judea. Instead, yet another dream led him to Nazareth (2:22).

This outlines the first two chapters of Matthew. When chapter three opens, nearly thirty years have passed.

II. Peculiarities in the Story.

Peculiarities in this case mean that there are unusual ways Matthew tells about Jesus. We need to take note of these peculiarities.

(1) Joseph has four dreams from God.
• An angel tells him to take Mary as his wife. Do not be afraid. Her child is of the Holy Spirit (1:20-21).
• An angel tells Joseph to flee with Mary and the baby to Egypt (2:13).
• When Herod died, "an angel of the Lord" told Joseph to take the family back to Israel (2:19).
• "Being warned in a dream," Joseph settled in Galilee instead of Judea (2:22).

Dreams appear often in the Bible. Jacob, Joseph, Daniel, and Paul either had dreams or could interpret them. There may be more to dreams than our generation is willing to admit. God has used them in the past.

(2) Joseph and Mary never speak a word in Matthew's birth narrative. A narrator tells the story. Mary is as much a bit player in Matthew's gospel as Joseph is a bit player in Luke's, but neither speaks in Matthew. God is the mover, speaker, planner, and preserver. God initiates all action in Matthew.

(3) Matthew does not give details. How long were Joseph, Mary, and Jesus in Bethlehem? How long did they stay in Egypt? Where did they go in Egypt? We are not told.

(4) Matthew's use of Scripture is puzzling. He uses Old Testament passages to buttress his story.
• Matthew never drops a Scripture from Mark or any other source. There are at least sixty-one in his gospel.
• Matthew is not trying to persuade "outsiders" Jesus is the Messiah; he is writing for insiders. "The conviction that Jesus is the Christ is the presupposition of his use of Scripture" (*The New Interpreter's Bible*, Vol. VIII, Nashville: Abingdon Press, 1995, 153).

• By our standards, Matthew is careless with his Old Testament quotations. Often they seem to have little connection with what he is illustrating. But by first-century Jewish standards, Matthew's use of Scripture is not only acceptable, it is extraordinarily effective.

III. An Interpretation of the Story.

The lesson title, "When Kingdoms Collide," seems a stretch for the text, but Matthew wrote with a world view in mind. Understanding Matthew's perspective helps us grasp the power in this lesson.

(1) Jesus always moved on a world stage. From birth, this babe born in Bethlehem was destined for greatness. Herod, a person of enormous consequence, noticed and feared the birth of Jesus.

Wise Men came "from the East." They were Gentiles. Jesus and the gospel he preached was not meant for Jews alone. Jesus would make his mark among Gentiles.

Jonah is one Old Testament illustration that the gospel was for the world. But that gospel was suppressed, and a near hatred for Gentiles became Judaism's public face. Jesus would change that.

(2) Jesus has always threatened a "Herod" kind of mind. Throughout history there have been too many Herods—cruel people who do murder and meanness as habit. People who are hard and cruel always recognize Jesus as their natural enemy. They are hard; he was merciful and forgiving. They are jealous; he was self-emptying and given to service. They want more; Jesus gave more. They excluded; Jesus included. They think of the present; Jesus kept eternity in view. They set themselves up as gods; Jesus was of the very nature of God. And he wanted the commitment and loyalty only God can ask.

Jesus did not let this side of his nature go without comment. Jesus warned his followers that discipleship would be hazardous duty. "Blessed are you when people revile you and persecute you..." (Mt 5:11). So when Herod murdered innocent children to try to kill Jesus, it was only the first of a pattern. Jesus prompts strong feelings.

(3) Jesus has always been preserved to God's purposes. Joseph didn't save Jesus from Herod. God did. Joseph obeyed God, and obedience is Joseph's virtue. God stepped in, gave a plan to rescue, and would not allow the mission of Jesus to be cut short. Matthew saw the big picture; and in the big picture was the hand of God preserving, protecting, extending Jesus to his mission.

Much of my preaching has been done from a small vantage point. I looked so intently at my text (usually just a few verses) until I lost the big picture. Matthew never did. He saw the whole picture. God sent Jesus to save. God would not let Herod or Pilate, Pharisees or Judas, popes or denominations, self-seeking preachers or unlearned teachers keep Jesus from his assigned task. Through all these people and roadblocks God has moved to enlarge and preserve Jesus and the people who bear his name. I think Matthew had a vision of a world-wide Church. He saw the spread of the gospel. His gospel is written with an eye to a Christ who would overpower and rise above a Caesar. It was unthinkable in his time. From our perspective it doesn't seem strange at all. Caesar is still studied; Jesus is worshipped.

When you see what Matthew was doing, our title doesn't seem out-of-touch at all. Kingdoms have collided and they still do. A Kingdom of peace still wrestles against the kingdoms of this world. A Kingdom of fairness still wrestles against all kingdoms of greed. Just like Matthew said it would be.

Notes

Notes